snoopy's

facts & fun book about seashores

Based on the
Charles M. Schulz Characters

Random House   New York

Designed by Terry Flanagan

Copyright © 1980 by United Feature Syndicate, Inc. Produced in association with Charles M. Schulz Creative Associates. All rights reserved under International and Pan-American Copyright Conventions. Published in the United States by Random House, Inc., New York, and simultaneously in Canada by Random House of Canada Limited, Toronto. Library of Congress Cataloging in Publication Data: Main entry under title: Snoopy's facts & fun book about seashores. SUMMARY: Snoopy and his friends explore the many different things one can observe and do at the seashore. 1. Seashore biology—Juvenile literature. 2. Seashore—Juvenile literature. [1. Seashore. 2. Seashore biology] I. Schulz, Charles M. II. Series. QH95.7.S58 574.909′4′6 79-23362 ISBN 0-394-84298-7; 0-394-94298-1 (lib. bdg.)
Manufactured in the United States of America   1 2 3 4 5 6 7 8 9 0

Smart sunbathers arrive at the seashore
early in the morning. The sun hasn't had a
chance to heat up the sand yet. No one
likes to walk on hot sand!

Even on a hot day, the ocean water feels cool. Water takes longer to heat up than air.

Notice how salty the water tastes.
There really is salt in ocean water.
You can see it left on your skin after
the water dries up.

The salt in ocean water helps you float.

On some beaches, you can see surf-casters fishing from the shore. They throw their fishing lines far out into the waves.

If you turn your back to the water, you might see sand dunes. These are big hills of sand blown there by the wind.

Sandpipers scurry along the beach, close to the water. They scoot away from the waves just in time!

On windy or stormy days, waves get very big at ocean beaches. Surfers like to ride the big waves on surfboards.

Seaweed are plants that live in the ocean. Most kinds hold tightly to rocks underwater. You might find some floating or washed ashore after the waves have torn them loose.

Snorkelers swim underwater, looking at the ocean bottom. They breathe through a snorkel tube that sticks out above the water.

Waves wash rocks, driftwood, and pieces of glass up onto the beach. They have been polished smooth from bouncing around in the ocean. Collecting them is fun.

Once you start collecting things on the beach, don't forget to include seashells. A seashell used to be part of a live ocean animal. The hard shell made a safe covering for the animal's soft parts.

If your beach is near warm ocean waters, you might find empty conch shells. When you hold one up to your ear, you hear a sound like the ocean.

Clam shells were once part of animals called clams. Some clams are good to eat. You can dig for them in the sand under shallow water. Clams burrow into the sand so that rough waves won't hurt them.

A whelk is a kind of snail that lives in the ocean. Finding its empty shell is easy. But you have to be lucky to find a string of whelk egg cases. Inside each case is a group of tiny whelk eggs.

Barnacles are small animals with very hard shells. They fasten themselves to rocks or boats and hold on tight.

Crabs skitter across the sand looking for food. Be careful of the crab's strong claws. They can pinch!

Is that a snail with claws? No! It's a hermit crab. Hermit crabs live in shells that used to belong to other animals.

A horseshoe crab looks scary, but it won't hurt anyone. It's not really a crab at all. It is a cousin of the spider. Like a spider, a horseshoe crab has eight walking legs.

In ocean bays, you can often see jellyfish floating in shallow water. It's easy to see how they got their name. They really **do** look like blobs of jelly.

YOU DON'T SUPPOSE THAT'S HOW THEY MAKE JELLY, DO YOU?

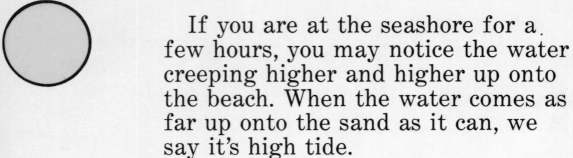

If you are at the seashore for a few hours, you may notice the water creeping higher and higher up onto the beach. When the water comes as far up onto the sand as it can, we say it's high tide.

After high tide, the water starts to creep back down again. The beach looks much bigger. When the water goes as far back as it can, we say it's low tide.

At low tide, small pools of water are left among the rocks. Fish and other sea creatures are trapped in the tide pools. They can't return to the ocean until high tide.

Sometimes starfish are left in tide pools. Most starfish have five arms. But some starfish, called sun stars, have as many as 14 arms!

At the end of the day, you may see fishing boats bringing in their catch. Some fishing people have nets bulging with fish. Others have lobsters collected in lobster pots or traps.

Gulls circle overhead, looking for extra fish or garbage scraps.

By nightfall, you and the other sunbathers are on your way home. The only sounds at the seashore are the wind and the waves.